HOW TO FOLLOW-UP

YOUR PROSPECT

Step by step
From Newbies to Professionals

SAI JAMES

How To Follow-up Your Prospect: Step by step From Newbies to Professionals

Table of Contents

Introduction

One of the skills every novice sales person should know is how to follow-up on a prospect the right way. Not following up on a prospect properly will most likely make you lose the sale, or worse give you and your organization a bad reputation to the prospect. In this book, we'll teach you the right and most efficient way of following up on a prospect.

As you read along, you'll learn different techniques in making follow-ups to prospects, either via telephone, voice mail, email, or a person-to-person conversation. The skills that this book will impart are keys to becoming a truly trustworthy and successful sales professional. Thank you and we hope that you enjoy this book.

Chapter 1: Prospecting - Building A Solid Foundation

One crucial thing that most sales people overlook is that in order for you to successfully follow up on a prospect, you must learn how to find that prospect in the first place. The foundation to conducting successful prospect follow-ups is to have an abundance of prospects to follow up with in the first place.

Remember, it doesn't matter how good a sales person is at building rapport, asking questions, managing objections, or presenting the product or service if they don't have any prospects at all. Prospecting is crucial to an illustrious career in sales.

So what is prospecting? Prospecting is basically the act seeking out potential customers from the general public. Prospecting, when done in the most friendly and courteous way, can be done almost anywhere. You can look for prospects in social functions, during a plane ride, a Parent-Teacher Association meeting, etc.

There's always an opportunity to prospect wherever people are gathered. Do keep in mind, however, that this doesn't mean that you ambush everyone at the train station, or hound everybody at the airport, or corner everyone who's out on the golf course like a creep.

To be a skilled prospector, you must first have a unique interest in other people. Try to strike up a friendly conversation regarding events or occurrences that you and your prospect are experiencing. Listen intently to everything that your prospect is saying. During the conversation, it is very likely that you'll uncover a need for the product or service that you're offering and tell them about it.

So how does one become an effective prospector? Well, for starters, you must make it a point to talk to at least three people that you do not know every day. Have a conversation with them and constantly look for ways to uncover a need that your product or service may address. Keep in mind that practice makes perfect. It will take a certain amount of time to become a truly effective prospector. But once you master it, you'll reap the benefit of having an endless prospect pipeline.

Great Places for Lead Mining

Now we all know that prospects originate from numerous lead sources. It is therefore critical to know what are the best places to source or mine leads for prospecting. Below are five great places to mine leads for prospecting:

1. The "warm" market — It doesn't matter whether the sales person is a novice or a veteran. The first person the sales professional will tell about the product or service that he or she is offering are their families, friends, acquaintances, former bosses, colleagues, etc. For the sales professional, these are the people who he or she has already built rapport with. These are people who the sales professional knows on a personal level.

2. Cold Calls — So what are cold calls? These are calls made by the sales professional to people who they've never met before and are not entirely clear whether they're interested in the product or service that you're offering. This is one of the hardest places to mine leads from.

   Most of the time, the person on the other line will reject the call and refuse to speak to you once they find out your making a sales call. Cold calling is the epitome of lead mining, literally. Cold calling is like picking at rocks deep in the mine shaft until you strike the gold.

3. Referrals – This is one of the easiest places to mine leads. Referrals are basically people who your current customers think might be also interested in the service or product that you're offering. This is considered the best place to get leads fast and convert them to existing customers. Why? Because trust is automatically established, albeit partially, between you and the new prospect through an introduction made by your existing customer.

4. Current Customers – These are the people who you currently have a business relationship with; a customer. Current customers can be a great prospect once again. Since you've already provided them with a great product or service, you have already built rapport and trust with these people, thus making them inclined to get more or a totally different product or service from you. This is one of the reasons why maintaining a good long-term relationship with your customers is crucial to a successful career in sales.

5. Niche Market – Mining leads from the niche market is basically leveraging the competition to gain a significant number of prospects. In other words, you strike up a mutually beneficial partnership—a combined effort—to sell into each other's prospect pool so generate business.

Note that the best lead source may vary from sales person to sales person. If one sales person is getting good quality prospects from cold calling, it doesn't mean you will too. That sales person might have excellent cold calling skills, while you do not. So to find which of the aforementioned sources work best for you, find out which particular lead source most of your prospects come from. Assess your situation, find out which of the aforementioned sources give you quality prospects and concentrate on those.

Identifying the Right Prospect

As a sales professional, it is your job to root out which prospect is worth investing time with. Because let's face it, not every person who you come across actually want or need your product. And even if they do need your service or product, the question is do they have the authority to make that buying decision and do they have to ability to make the financial investment to finalize the sale.

Therefore, it is important that you generate a prospect profile based on your current customer base. What are you current customers like? What are their similarities? Do they come from the same industry? Are their job titles similar to each other? Are they small business owners or big companies?

Remember, you must also consider your company and yourself when generating an ideal prospect profile. Try to determine whether a certain type of prospect or customer would be profitable for the company. Make sure that you are pinpointing customers which you think will give you the best return on your effort and time invested. Qualified prospects usually have these three main characteristics:

1. Unmet need
2. Ability to pay
3. Authority to make the buying decision

If any one of these characteristics is missing, then there's no point in pushing the sale forward. Pushing the sale forward to an unqualified prospect not only wastes time, but also creates tension and distrust in your and whichever company your represent. It is therefore considered good sales practice to disqualify a customer or prospect and move on to the next.

Keep in mind that it doesn't matter whether you think you have the best service or product in the whole world. There are people out there who couldn't care less. What you need to do—your job—is to root them out quickly so you can help the people who actually need what you're offering.

Chapter 2: Essential Prospect Follow-up Skills

Telephone

Telephone call handling skills in sales is something that every sales professional shouldn't take for granted. Just like life in the real world, nothing is easy about the skillful utilization of the telephone as a basic sales business tool. Your listening skills are crucial every time you are making a sales follow-up over the telephone.

Remember, the prospect on the other end of the call have nothing else to go on except your voice and what you're actually saying. Therefore, it is of utmost importance that you approach any sales telephone conversation knowing how to establish an excellent telephone presence.

1. Telephone basic number one is Attitude. Here's a point that every professional sales person should take note of: Your attitude is paramount. You must project a winning, cooperative, can-do attitude at all times. The key to maintaining a positive attitude is maintaining the perception

that every call is an opportunity, not an annoyance.

You know you can hear "attitudes" over the phone. Your customer or prospects can tell if you are smiling, annoyed, or happy. Whatever attitude you have is clearly projected over the phone. So put a smile in your voice by putting a smile on your face.

2. Telephone basic number two is Preparation. Have what you need before you begin making your follow-up calls. Have pens, pencils, paper, a resource material, computer, anything you're going to need immediately available. When you are making a call, understand your sales objective and leave nothing to chance. Know clearly what you're trying to achieve.

   Is it a face-to-face appointment to follow-up a sale, or to gain permission to send more information? Whatever the objective, you need to have it clearly in your mind before you make the call. Making a call with a "let's see where it takes us" attitude will not consistently take you where you want to go.

3. Telephone basic number three is Getting Started. Every sales

professional making follow up calls over the telephone must remember that the first 10 to 15 seconds sets the tone for the entire conversation. If you have a spiel from which you do not digress, then even the most challenging phone calls will start off on the right foot and continue smoothly. Always try to include the following three elements in the beginning of your call:

- Greeting - Your company may mandate how you greet your customers. If not, create a snappy greeting that will set a positive tone.

- Clearly Identify Yourself and your Company - Do not mumble or rush through this. Telling the prospect on the other line who you are and what your organization is all about requires a little bit of finesse, or else the prospect would brush you off and hang up. Also, the person on the other end of the phone has to process what they are hearing. Therefore, be patient and give them time to digest whatever information you've just given them.

- State the Objective of your Call – This is the part where you use a general benefit statement to gain someone's interest.

4. Telephone basic number four is to remember to keep it professional. This refers to the fact that as a professional sales person, you have to be capable of conveying a professional presence over the phone. You can't afford to follow-up on a sale over the phone with a "proper and rehearsed" spiel only to accidentally hang up on a customer or prospect when trying to transfer them or put them on hold.

There are numerous common events that are likely to occur during the course of an average telephone call. Take the time to become proficient at them. We all know people who have worked in a given office situation for years and still don't have any idea of how to transfer or conference a call. Learn the system that you work with so that you give the customer the security of knowing they are dealing with a professional.

5. Telephone basic number five is to be aware of lasting impressions. The last thing the person on the other end hears will possibly be the only lasting impression you will leave. Leave a good impression. The end of any call should include a thank you. Show courtesy and appreciation for the person

spending their time with you. A final confirmation of information delivered and a friendly goodbye are action required.

Learn How to Use the Voicemail for Follow-ups Effectively

Every professional sales person would agree that recent advancements in technology have changed the way people do business. As time went by, people have become accustomed to having instant solutions, instantly having information at their fingertips, and accessibility to the answers they seek. To keep your prospect's or customer's attention, constant communication is a must. Considering the plethora of technologies available to a sales professional such as your own self, staying connected with prospect or customer should be easier. In some cases, however, this is not entirely the truth.

One specific technology that every sales person would encounter when making follow-up calls is the voice mail. When you make a call to a prospect or a previous customer, chances are great that you'll get the voice mail. This is especially true of you're making a cold call to a prospect and you don't know the time of day that they're available.

Getting the voice mail might be extremely frustrating considering that despite leaving a voice mail message with your contact information, only a few people actually get back to you. So the main question is: how do you use the voice mail effectively when making follow-ups on a prospect? Well, the key is to leave a voice mail message that will pique your prospect's curiosity enough to get them to call you back posthaste.

Below are important points to consider when leaving a compelling sales follow-up voice mail:

- First, learn how to show your enthusiasm through your voice. Remember that you're a sales professional who wants to help them address a problem or a need. Let your prospect on the other line feel your enthusiasm through your voice. You got to do this while clearly stating your name, your organization, how they can reach you, and how your product or service will benefit that specific prospect.

- Second, keep it short and simple. Never ever leave a voice mail that is more than 20 seconds long. If you leave a voice mail message that is too long, you run the risk of the prospect deleting your voice mail message even before it finishes.

- Lastly, make your voice mail message unique. Never ever leave a generic voice mail message; a message that sounds and feels the same as any other message that the prospect may have waiting when he gets back. Leave an upbeat message that piques your prospect's interest at the shortest amount of time. Try to make him curious, but never give all the details so that he will call you back to know more. Again, do not forget to insert some general benefit statements regarding your product or service.

Learning How to Use Email for Effective Follow-ups

Today, emails are used extensively in business. It is one of the major modes of communication in any business setting. So how do you use emails effectively when making sales follow-ups? For starters, if you're following-up on a current customer, you can make use of the email to tell them about a new product or service that you have that might work well with a product or service that they've already purchased.

Make sure that every email you send contains information that they can use for their business in relation to what you offer. Do not incessantly send emails with the aim of just asking them to make more purchases. It will make you sound pushy and make you look like you're just in it for the money. Also, this will surely annoy the prospect and delete your email right away.

Sending spam emails will eventually put you and your organization in bad light with the prospect or customer. Instead, try to develop an email that sounds and feels like you want to help with their problem first, and sell the product or service second. The great thing about these emails is that after you've invested time and effort creating them, they can be used over and over for any prospect. Think of it as making an effective email follow-up template.

Here are a few email ideas on how to make an effective sales email:

- First, make sure that you have the right contact/email list for that particular email that you're sending. It would be very awkward if you sent an email selling basketball gear to an email list consisting of die-hard soccer fans. Make sure your email caters specifically to the group of customers or prospects you're sending to.

- Second, always give your customer or prospect a reason to make a purchase. Offer special discounts, offer a premium product or service at regular price, give a free upgrade, anything that would make the person want to reply back to you and take advantage of your offer.

  Do not, however, flood the prospect with an overwhelming list of offers that they'll get confused on which product to choose. Studies show that offering one or two products does an exemplary job of hooking the prospect or customer in, compared to offering multiple products all at once.

- Third, make your emails catchy. Just like voice mail, you have a narrow window to capture the prospect or customer's interest. Try starting the mail with a catchy benefit statement that will get them hooked and want to read more. For example, you can try starting your email with, "How does saving 50% on fuel cost sound to you?" You can then tell them about the specifics of the offer and how they can take advantage.

- Fourth, make sure your email sounds and looks professional. Never ever send an email that's riddled with horrendous grammar and misspelled words. Try to include your company logo at the heading of every email. Making use of background colors is fine as long as there's not too much of it. Put yourself in the prospect's shoes and ask yourself whether you would read the email that came from you.

- Lastly, include any information that would help your prospect or customer in their business. Your emails should always be about you selling something. Keep in mind that your main goal is to keep the information pathway with your prospect fresh. Send them useful tidbits of information even if it is not directly related to what you and your company is offering.

There are many articles online that may prove beneficial to your prospects business. And it is your job to make them feel that you value them by sending to them things that might help them in the long run.

Chapter 3: Try and Try Until you Succeed

Research have shown that 46% of sales professionals today asked the customer or prospect for the sale once, never makes a follow-up and then quits. 24% asked for the sale once, makes a follow-up once, and then gives up. 14% asked for the sale three times before giving up, and then only 12% asked for the sale four times before putting their hands up and giving up.

In other words, 96% of sales professionals today quit asking for the sale or follow-up after the fourth attempt. However, another research show that around 70% of all successful sales closes was achieved after the fifth attempt.

How many times do you ask for the sale or make a follow-up on a prospect? If your answer is less than five, then you should consider going back to that customer or prospect and try again. Most sales people have this fear of coming off as an extremely pushy and high-pressure sales professional when they ask for the sale once or twice.

While it is true that you do not want to annoy a prospect or customer by being pushy, asking for the sale for more than five times in a polite and unintrusive manner will never make you look like one.

Think about it this way: In a baseball game, every time a pitcher rejects a baseball, the ball is thrown back to the umpire who puts it back in his ball pouch together with the other balls. As the game moves on, that same ball would be given to the pitcher and is used to pitch the game. It is very rare that the pitcher will reject the same ball twice.

The same thing applies with your offer. The prospect will look at what you offer in a different light each time you present it to them when making a follow-up and asking for the sale. Just like how the baseball umpire offers the same ball to the pitcher, so you must offer the same service or product to the prospect or customer multiple of times.

The only reason why you would have a problem asking for the sale or making a follow-up again and again is either you don't believe in the product that you're selling, or you don't expect to close the sale at all with that particular prospect.

Every time you make a follow-up and present you product or service again, make sure you give new features, reasons, benefits, and functions to the prospect in order for them to make the buying decision today. Giving your prospect new information about the product or service allows them to reevaluate their previous decision and make a new decision based on the new information that just came into light.

More often than not, sales professionals do not follow-up because they don't want to hear the dreaded "NO" answer from the prospect or customer. If you have this kind of mindset, you definitely want to give evaluate yourself. Relive your initial sales presentation with the prospect and debrief yourself. Ask yourself whether you asked for the sale. If not, why didn't you follow up accordingly?

If some of your answers are, "... the timing just wasn't right," "The prospect was distracted," "... there were too many people around," or "... she needed to take a breather and think things through," realize these are often excuses for not asking for the order. Don't misunderstand. There are occasions when it's wise to back away and return another day, especially if the amount of investment you're asking the prospect to make is significant.

However, in an overwhelming majority of the cases, you need to be honest with yourself and admit you're just making excuses for yourself and you need to ask for the order. To learn how to ask for the order every time, count how many times you asked for the order with each prospect today.

If it's less than five, then tomorrow, commit to yourself that you'll just try one more time with each prospect. Keep stretching yourself so that you know when you lose a sale, you know it was not because you didn't give it your best effort.

Conclusion

Following up on a prospect may be hard for some sales professional to do. However, keep in mind that most of the successful sales closes occur after the fifth attempt. When doing your follow-ups, try to act professional, courteous, not intrusive, and always add value to what you are offering by presenting the prospect or customer with new information. As what we have said earlier, new information about a product or service might just be the key to unlocking the customer's hesitation and objection in going through with the order.

With that in mind, always keep making follow-ups and never hesitate to approach the customer or prospect with renewed enthusiasm. Once you exude enthusiasm in your approach, it is likely that they will share that enthusiasm as well. Whether you're following up on a prospect via the telephone, voice mail, email, or in person, always remember to help the customer or prospect first, and sell your product or service second.

We would like to thank you for purchasing this book and we hope that you've learned a lot about how to properly follow-up on a sales from a customer or prospect. We hope that you will be able to increase your productivity with the skills indicated in this book. Please feel free to share this book with a colleague so that you may be able to help them in their sales career as well.

Thank you.